crafting*on*the*go

shells

crafting*on*the*go

shells

sixth&spring
books

sixth&spring
books

233 Spring Street
New York, NY 10013

Library of Congress Cataloging-in-Publication Data

Crafting on the go! Shells / [Editor, Trisha Malcolm]
    p. cm.
    ISBN 1-931543-34-8
    1. Shellcraft. I. Malcolm, Trisha, 1960- II. Crafting on the go!

TT862.C724 2003
    745.55--dc21   2002042943

Manufactured in China

1 3 5 7 9 10 8 6 4 2

First Edition

contents

introduction

Who among us can resist beachcombing for seashells on a breezy summer day? It's a childhood pastime that carries on into adulthood. As kids we took endless delight in scooping them up out of the sand, amazed by their very existence and eager to share bucketfuls with sunbathers back on the beach blanket. As grownups we tuck the few that catch our fancy into our pockets, bringing them home with us as mementos of a day in the sun.

But what is our fascination with shells? Perhaps it's their one-of-a-kind beauty. Each is unique— a tiny treasure sculpted and colored by nature, each one perfect in its own way. Shells have a soothing beauty. Looking at them calls up memories of lazy weekends by the sea, the warmth of the sun and the salty scent of an ocean breeze.

Shells lend themselves to endless crafting possibilities. They can be scattered across tabletops, artfully arranged in glass bowls, pressed into candle wax, set into tiles or glued into intricate sculptures. No matter how we use them, their very presence creates a peaceful and contemplative oasis. The ideas on the following pages are meant to inspire. Use them to preserve your own collection of seaside treasures—and as incentive for collecting more.

shell seeking

Living by the beach has its benefits, not the least of which is the availability of seashells. If you live inland, the following resources are helpful in finding the right shells for the project at hand.

Craft stores often sell small bags of shells, look for them in the jewelry-making sections. Internet sites, such as www.usshell.com, have abundant supplies and offer a great assortment. Best of all, the shells are delivered right to your doorstep.

If you're the adventurous type, there are plenty of places to collect shells while soaking up the sun. Florida's west coast has places like Sanibel Island, which is famous for its shelling. However, wherever you go, make sure to find out if shelling is permitted.

Jingle Shell

Olive

Nassarius Phyrrus

Dyed Trochus

Cerithium

Tonna Tessalata

Murex

Auger

Kings Crown

Seahorse

Ark

Ram's Horn

11

Chocolate Clam

Strawberry Top

Brown Littorina

Dove

Littorina

Keyhole
Sand Dollar

White Natica

Sea Glass

Dyed Turbo

Cowrie

Starfish

Babylonia Alrolata

White Auger

White Chula

Turitella

Pecten

Coquina

Mule Ear Abalone

Green Littorina

Pearlized Umbonium

Dyed Baby Ark

Baby Ark

13

working with shells

Select unbroken shells for decorating. Only collect shells that have been washed up on the beach or shore. Never remove a shell from its natural habitat—there may be a creature living inside. While shells saved from steamed or boiled dinners work well for crafting, shells left over from baking or broiling are usually too brittle to work with.

To prepare shells for craft projects, scrape away any barnacles with a small, sharp knife. Wipe away surface sand and dirt with a damp cloth. To remove stubborn build-up, soak shells overnight in detergent and water. The next day, rinse the shells and scrape them again or scrub them with a brush. Bathroom cleaners with lime are also very good for cleaning shells.

To whiten discolored shells and remove bacteria, soak them in a solution of one part bleach and three parts water for about six hours. Be careful not to soak the shells for too long as their natural color will fade and they will become brittle. Rinse them thoroughly with cold water.

To clean openings in small shells, pry out sand and dirt with a toothpick or small utensil, then wipe them clean with a cotton swab.

Glue will not stick to wet or damp shells. Allow shells to dry thoroughly—several hours or even overnight—before using them for a craft project. Once dry, shells can be attached with craft, tacky or hot glue.

Spray finished projects with a clear gloss acrylic sealer to protect the shells and give your project a polished effect.

circles in the sand

Whether at the beach or miles from shore, a cheery shell wreath makes a fresh summer door accent.

materials

- One 14" (35cm) Styrofoam® wreath form

- E6000® multi-purpose adhesive

- Two dozen large and medium Chocolate Clam shells

- One dozen pink Pecten shells

- Four dozen assorted-size Baby Ark shells

- Eight dozen assorted-size Littorina shells

1 Working in a circular motion from the top outer edge of the wreath, glue the large Chocolate Clam shells onto the form, facing outward.

2 Repeat with the medium Chocolate Clam shells, placing them so they face outward and slightly overlap the larger shells underneath. Let dry.

3 Glue Pink Pecten shells along the inner edge of the wreath form, facing toward the center of the wreath.

4 Glue Baby Ark shells over the pink Pecten shells on the inside of the wreath to fill in any spaces through which the form is showing.

5 Using assorted-size Littorina shells, fill in around the outer edge of the wreath between the Clam shells.

6 Repeat with the smallest Littorina shells until the entire wreath form is covered; let dry.

night light

Mini conch shells make a stunning holder for a pillar candle. Scatter several around the room for a truly illuminating experience.

materials

- 6" (15cm) terra cotta flowerpot saucer
- Pillar candle
- E6000® multi-purpose adhesive
- Five dozen Littorina shells

1 Place the pillar candle in the center of the terra cotta saucer.

2 Glue the Littorina shells to the saucer in a circular pattern, starting at the bottom, and working out until both the inside and the outer edge of the saucer are completely covered.

3 Let the first layer of shells dry once it is complete. Add two more layers to form a ring; let dry.

treasure chest

Preserve letters, ticket stubs and other mementos in this keepsake box encrusted with shells and sea glass.

materials

- **Small unfinished-wood box with hinges**
- **Beacon™ Gem-Tac™ glue**
- **Glue brush**
- **Three Kings Crown shells**
- **Four dozen Baby Ark shells**
- **12 dozen Dyed Tiny Trochus shells**
- **Bits of sea glass**

1 Brush a layer of Gem-Tac™ onto the top of the box.

2 Set the shells and sea glass onto the box, starting with the larger shells and filling in any spaces with the smaller ones. Let dry for at least 30 minutes.

3 Repeat the process on the front and sides until the box is covered. As you fill in these areas, make sure that the sea glass and shells do not cover the box opening and prevent the lid from closing properly.

wake-up call

Serve a bit of sand and surf with breakfast by layering a wood tray with an assortment of shells and Starfish.

- Unfinished-wood tray
- Acrylic paint in peach
- Small paintbrush
- Resin kit
- One Seahorse
- Four medium Starfish
- Assorted small-shell mix
- One dozen small Auger and Dove shells
- Four dozen small Pearlized Umbonium shells
- Craft glue

1 Paint the tray with two coats of peach acrylic, letting the paint dry after each coat.

2 Working in a well-ventilated area, pour a ½" (1.3cm) layer of resin into the tray following manufacturer's instructions.

3 Place the Seahorse in the center of the tray and one Starfish in each corner. Arrange the small shells in the tray as desired.

4 When the first layer of resin is dry (approximately 20 minutes), pour on a second layer, about another ½" (1.3cm), to completely cover the shell design.

5 Let the tray dry overnight in a well-ventilated area.

6 Glue Pearlized Umbonium shells along the interior edge of the tray as pictured; let dry.

plant it pretty

A wood planter painted a lovely shade of blue complements hydrangea or other delicate blooms when accented with a variety of sand-hued shells.

- **Unfinished-wood planter**
- **Acrylic paint in periwinkle blue**
- **Small foam brush**
- **Hot-glue gun and glue sticks**
- **Assorted Pecten, Cowrie and Coquina shells**

1 Paint the planter with two coats of periwinkle blue acrylic, letting the paint dry after each coat.

2 Turn the planter on its side and hot-glue the shells onto the front as desired. Allow the planter to dry completely before filling it with plants.

sand swept

A pretty pattern of shells, sea glass and a Sand Dollar creates a stepping stone that will be a striking addition to any garden.

materials

- **Plaster stepping-stone kit**
- **One large Keyhole Sand Dollar**
- **Five brown Turitella shells**
- **Two dozen assorted Olive and Cowrie shells**
- **One dozen Coquina shells**
- **24 pieces of sea glass**

1 Following the manufacturer's directions on the stepping-stone kit, mix the plaster and fill the stepping-stone form.

2 Push the Sand Dollar, shells and sea-glass pieces into the surface of the wet plaster, arranging them as desired.

3 Allow the stepping stone to dry completely then carefully remove it from the form.

weight watchers

Hosting an outdoor party? Keep the linens from blowing away these beachy tablecloth weights.

materials

Four small drapery rings with clips

Hot-glue gun and glue sticks

Eight Pecten shells

1 Hot-glue one Pecten shell to either side of a drapery ring so the ring is sandwiched between the shells. (Be sure the shells used for each clip are similar in size and shape.) Let dry completely.

2 Hot-glue shells to the three remaining drapery rings in the same manner.

3 Attach the clips at intervals around the hem of a tablecloth.

picture perfect

materials

Small unfinished-wood frame

Mod Podge® glue

Glue brush

Sand

E6000® multi-purpose adhesive

Six dozen Baby Ark shells

Four dozen assorted-size Coquina shells

Assorted small Cerithium, Turitella, Cowrie, Kings Crown and Dyed Trochus shells

A wood frame embellished with shells and tiny Starfish makes the perfect showcase for vacation snapshots. Dress it up with a shell "rose" in each corner.

1 Remove the backing and glass from the frame.

2 Spread an even coat of Mod Podge® onto the frame.

3 Pour sand over the frame to cover it completely. Let the glue dry, then shake the frame to remove the excess sand.

4 Starting at the outside, glue the shells in a flower pattern in two corners of the frame. Work slowly, allowing the shells to set and dry before layering.

5 Cover the rest of the frame with a single layer of Baby Ark shells.

6 Glue assorted small shells on top of the Baby Ark shells as desired. Let dry completely.

7 Replace the frame's backing and glass.

ocean view

**Set a glass bowl brimming with shells and
sea glass on a side table or countertop for a
daily reminder of sea's beauty.**

materials

- **Small decorative bowl**

- **Assorted small-shell mix**

- **Sea glass**

- **Scented oil**

1 In the bowl, combine the shells, sea glass and a
few drops of scented oil.

2 Stir the contents of the bowl occasionally to
release the scent and refresh the oil weekly.

making waves

A foam cone covered with shells is a clever
twist on the traditional topiary. Set in a
galvanized bucket and surrounded with seaside
treasures, it makes a perfect accent for a
sun porch or sitting room.

materials

**One Styrofoam®
topiary form**

**Six dozen assorted-size
Baby Ark shells**

**E6000® multi-
purpose adhesive**

Galvanized bucket

Spanish moss

1 Starting at the top, glue the Baby Ark shells to
the topiary form in a spiral pattern, working
your way to the bottom.

2 Fill in any remaining spaces with smaller Baby
Ark shells until the form is completely covered.

3 Once the topiary is dry, place it in the container.

4 Fill in the areas around the topiary base with
Spanish moss.

beach balls

Suspended from satin ribbons, these
shell-trimmed ornaments make an elegant
addition to the holiday tree or a
charming year-round window accent.

materials

(for one ornament)

One 4" (10cm)
Styrofoam® ball

Mod Podge® glue

Sand

One ornament hook

Assorted small-shell mix

Two paper plates

Double-faced satin
ribbon in desired width
and color

1 Pour a generous amount of Mod Podge® onto
a paper plate. Pour the sand onto a separate
paper plate.

2 Roll the Styrofoam® ball in the glue to cover the
entire surface.

3 Roll the ball in sand until it is completely coated.

4 Stick an ornament hook into the top of the ball
and allow the sand to dry.

5 Glue assorted small shells onto the sand-covered
ball and let dry. Thread a length of satin ribbon
through the ornament hook and hang as desired.

6 Thread a length of ribbon through the ornament
hook and hang the ball as desired.

name calling

Set a festive summer table with place card holders crafted from shells of varying sizes.

- **Four brown Ram's Horn shells**
- **Eight small Coquina shells**
- **Four place cards**
- **Hot-glue gun and glue sticks**

1 Put a small amount of glue at the center-top of one brown Ram's Horn shell.

2 Place two small Coquina shells slightly apart in the glue, with the wide ends down and facing each other. Allow to dry.

3 Repeat the process for each of the three remaining place card holders.

4 Put the place cards into the holders and arrange them on a table as desired.

seaside tote

Carry sunscreen, shades and other beach essentials in style with a pretty shell-trimmed straw tote.

materials

Purchased woven-straw handbag

15 Cowrie shells

Three Pearlized Umbonium shells

Beacon™ Fabri-Tac glue

1 Turn the bag on its side and glue the shells onto the front of the bag in a flower pattern, using the photograph as a guide. Use the Cowrie shells for the flower petals and the Pearlized Umbonium shells for the flower centers.

2 Allow the glue to dry and the shells to set before turning the bag right-side up.

mirror, mirror

Decorative White Natica shells lend a winsome touch to a round framed mirror.

materials

- **Large round framed mirror**

- **20 dozen White Natica shells**

- **Hot-glue gun and glue sticks**

1 Working in a circular pattern, hot-glue White Natica shells to the surface of the mirror frame.

2 Look carefully for any spaces where the frame is still visible. Hot-glue more shells to the frame until it is fully covered.

made in the shade

materials

- Small beige lampshade
- White acrylic paint
- Small foam brush
- 1" (2.5cm)-wide masking tape
- One dozen small Ram's Horn shells
- One dozen Baby Ark shells
- ½ cup assorted small-shell mix
- Hot-glue gun and glue sticks

An earth-toned shade trimmed with shell borders makes a perfect bedside lamp.

1 Tape vertical stripes onto the lampshade ¾" (2cm) apart. Paint white stripes in between the taped areas; let dry.

2 Alternating between shell types, hot-glue Baby Ark and Ram's Head shells along the top and bottom edges of the lampshade.

3 Fill in any remaining spaces with assorted small shells. Let the shade dry before placing it on a lamp.

Plain framed corkboard

Four large pink Pecten shells

Eight dozen Mule Ear Abalone shells

Six dozen White Chula shells

Four dozen Baby Ark shells

Hot-glue gun and glue sticks

surf's up

Need a spot to pin up postcards, notes or the business card from your favorite seafood joint? Frame a corkboard with a border of artfully arranged shells and secure keepsakes with sea-themed pushpins.

1 Hot-glue the pink Pecten shells to the corners of the corkboard frame.

2 Hot-glue the Mule Ear Abalone shells around the corkboard frame, leaving small spaces between them; let dry.

3 Hot-glue the White Chula shells in between the Mule Ear Abalone shells to fill the spaces.

4 Hot-glue the Baby Ark shells on top of the Mule Ear Abalone shells as pictured.

numbers game

Mark your beach house with flair.
Arrange shells into the numbers of your choosing.
Hang as is or glue to a rustic wooden board.

materials

Brass door numbers

E6000® multi-purpose adhesive

Baby Ark shells

Krylon® Acrylic Crystal Clear spray varnish

1 Glue the Baby Ark shells in an overlapping pattern to cover each door number. When covering the numbers, be careful not to obstruct the screw or nail holes that will be used to hang them.

2 Before hanging the finished numbers, spray them with clear acrylic varnish and let them dry.

taglines

A pretty homemade tag embellished with a small shell is the perfect way to complete a gift of love.

materials

Small plain gift tag with hole

One small shell

Craft glue

Raffia or ribbon

1 Glue the shell onto the gift tag.

2 Before writing a message, allow the tag to dry completely.

3 String raffia or ribbon through the hole in the tag and attach it to the gift.

happy
Birthday

dock lights

Votive holders studded with tiny shells radiate when arranged on tabletops or deck railings.

One pair of work gloves

Three glass
votive holders

Pre-mixed grout

Four dozen
small Pearlized
Umbonium shells

Votive candles

Cotton swabs

Small spatula

1 Put on the work gloves to protect your hands from the grout.

2 Spread a generous layer of grout onto the outside of one votive holder and press shells into the grout, placing them close together. Work in small sections since the grout dries quickly. If you get grout on a shell, dip a cotton swab in warm water then wash off the grout.

3 Repeat this process with the two remaining votives, then allow them to dry.

fancy footwork

Show off a perfect pedicure in breezy straw
flip-flops trimmed with tiny shells.
They partner perfectly with a tropical sarong
or a pair of cool Capris.

materials

**One purchased pair
of natural-fiber
flip-flop sandals**

**Beacon™ Fabri-Tac™
glue**

**Three dozen assorted-
size Cowrie shells**

1 Center and glue the Cowrie shells along the top
of the shoe straps in a straight line.

2 Allow the glue to dry completely before wearing
the sandals.

beach comber

Tame beach-bleached tresses with cute seashell-trimmed barrettes. You can give a similar treatment to headbands and ponytail holders.

materials

One small metal hair barrette

One small Cowrie shell

Two Baby Ark shells

Hot-glue gun and glue sticks

1 Hot-glue the Cowrie shell to the center of the barrette.

2 Hot-glue one Baby Ark shell onto the barrette on either side of the Cowrie shell.

3 Allow the glue to dry and the shells to set before handling.

note worthy

A single Starfish transforms a plain notebook into a journal perfect for recording vacation memories.

materials

materials

Pencil

Ruler

Kraft paper-covered journal

X-Acto® knife

One small Starfish

Craft glue

1 Draw a square, ¼" (.6cm) larger all around than the Starfish, on the cover of the journal.

2 Using the X-Acto® knife, carefully score along the outline of the square.

3 Working within the scored square, peel the layers of paper off of the book cover until the square is hollowed out.

4 Glue the Starfish into the square and allow the glue to dry.

cover up

A pale peach box trimmed with a decorative pattern of seaside beauties makes a quick and quirky cover for a boring tissue dispenser.

materials

- Unfinished-wood tissue-box cover

- Acrylic paint in peach

- Small foam brush

- Hot-glue gun and glue sticks

- Four large pink Pecten shells

- 10 dozen Baby Ark shells

- 10 dozen small Pearlized Umbonium shells

1 Paint the tissue-box cover with two coats of peach acrylic, letting the paint dry after each coat.

2 Hot-glue gun the shells onto the top and sides of the box as desired; let dry.

glow for it

Create a magical dance of light with pillar
candles surrounded by handcrafted shell candles.

materials

**One large Tonna
Tessalata shell**

One candle wick

Paraffin wax

1 Place the candle wick into the center of the
Tonna Tessalata shell.

2 Melt the paraffin wax following the
manufacturer's directions.

3 Holding the top of the wick so that it remains in
the center, pour the wax into the shell. Let cool.

4 Trim the wick to ¼" (.6cm) before burning
the candle.

table talk

Napkin rings crafted from miniature grapevine wreaths studded with shells recall a tangle of driftwood washed ashore.

materials

- One small grapevine wreath

- Assorted small-shell mix

- Hot-glue gun and glue sticks

1 Hot-glue assorted small shells to all sides of the grapevine wreath.

2 Let the napkin ring dry before inserting a napkin.

natural wonder

**Having cocktails on the deck? A shell-filled
paperweight prevents napkins from flying away
on breezy days and nights.**

materials

Resin kit

**Paperweight form or
small plastic bowl**

Assorted small-shell mix

1 Following the manufacturer's directions and
working in a well-ventilated area, pour a ½"
(1.3cm) layer of resin into the paperweight form
or plasic bowl.

2 Place the shells, face down, into the resin in a
desired pattern.

3 When the first layer of resin is dry (approximately
20 minutes), pour in a second layer of resin to
completely cover the shell pattern.

4 Let the resin dry in a well-ventilated area, then
remove the paperweight from the form.

bright ideas

Drape a doorway or deck railing with a lovely string of shining shells. Simply glue shells to the bulb bases and let the light shine through.

materials

One strand of string lights

10 each large White Natica, Ark, Pecten, Kings Crown and Cerithium shells

Hot-glue gun and glue sticks

1 With the lights unplugged, hot-glue one shell onto each plastic bulb socket so the bulb is covered. Be careful not to glue the shells to the bulbs themselves.

2 Let dry and continue down the string, alternating types of shells, until all the lights are covered.

basket basics

Bring the seaside to the table with a basket or
bowl covered in interesting shells.
Fill with fresh fruit or vegetables for
a charming kitchen accent.

- Wooden salad bowl

- Three dozen Baby
  Ark shells

- One cup Pearlized
  Umbonium shells

- One cup Cerithium shells

- One dozen Chula shells

- One dozen small White
  Natica shells

- Six small Keyhole
  Sand Dollars

- E6000® multi-purpose
  adhesive

1 Glue Keyhole Sand Dollars, Baby Ark, Cerithium
and Chula shells to the outside of the bowl in a
circular pattern.

2 Fill in any remaining spaces with clusters of
Pearlized Umbonium shells; let dry.

desk set

**A pen holder encrusted with tiny shells and
Sand Dollars brings a bit of the beach to the office.**

materials

**Unfinished-wood
pen holder**

**E6000® multi-
purpose adhesive**

**Two small Keyhole
Sand Dollars**

**Small Pearlized
Umbonium shells**

1 Center and glue one Keyhole Sand Dollar to each
side of the pen holder.

2 Glue the small shells to the pen holder until
all sides are completely covered. Let dry
before using.

ocean gem

11 Baby Ark shells

22 4mm pearl beads

22 head pins

33" to 39" (82.5cm to 97.5cm) 22-gauge silver wire

Silver link bracelet or 6.5" (16.5cm)-long piece of silver chain plus one clasp and one jump ring

Two small blocks of wood (one approximately 3" (7.5cm)-square and one approximately 3" x 6" (7.5cm x 15cm)

Drill with small drill bit

Round-nose jewelry pliers

Wire cutters

A silver chain strung with shells and pearls makes a beautiful bracelet to wear with any summer ensemble.

1 Place one Baby Ark shell, rough exterior side up, on the larger piece of wood with the widest part of the shell facing you. Put the smaller piece of wood on top of the shell so that it covers all but the tip. Apply enough pressure to the wood to hold the shell firmly in place.

2 With the drill set at the highest speed, make a hole in the tip of the shell by drilling into it at a 90-degree angle to the work surface. Repeat with the remaining shells.

3 Slip one pearl bead onto a head pin. Grasp the head pin with the pliers, about ⅛"(.3cm) from the bead, and bend the wire at a right angle. Wrap the wire back over the top jaw of the pliers, down the side and under the lower jaw to form a loop.

4 Holding the loop flat between the jaws of the pliers, wrap the wire around itself until it meets the pearl. Trim off the excess wire. Repeat with 10 more pearl beads and head pins.

5 Cut the silver wire into 3"(7.5cm) pieces. Thread each piece through the hole of a shell and bend the wire in the middle so the shell is hanging from the center.

6 Slip the loop of a pearl bead onto the wire on the interior side of each shell. Hold the ends of the wire together with the pliers and turn them until you have 1"(2.5cm) of twisted wire.

7 Loop the twisted wire around the pliers as in step three, slip the loop through a link of the bracelet or chain and close it.

8 Repeat with the remaining shells, attaching them to the bracelet or chain at ½"(1.3cm) intervals.

9 In the spaces between the shells, attach a pearl bead with a head pin, forming the loops as in step three, but slipping the wires through the bracelet links before closing the loops.

10 If you are not using a ready-made bracelet, thread a 3"(7.5cm) piece of wire through a pearl bead, form a loop at each end of the wire as in step three and pass one loop through the end of the chain and the other through the clasp before closing them. Repeat with another bead to attach the jump ring to the opposite end of the chain.

resources

Beacon Adhesives
Company Inc.
125 MacQuesten Parkway
South
Mount Vernon, NY 10550
914-699-3400
http://beaconcreates.com

Eclectic Products, Inc.
1075 Arrowsmith
Eugene, OR 97402
800-693-4667
www.eclecticproducts.com/
index.asp

Krylon Products Group
Cleveland, OH 44115
800-797-3332
www.krylon.com

Plaid Enterprises, Inc.
P.O. Box 7600
Norcross, GA 30091-7600
800-842-4197
www.plaidonline.com

Styrofoam Brand Products
The Dow Chemical
Company
P.O. Box 68
Chagrin Falls, OH 44022
440-247-4371
www.dow.com/styrofoam

US Shell
36451 Highway 100
Los Fresnos, TX 78566
956-554-4500
www.usshell.com

X-Acto Knives and Blades
Hunt Corporation
Customer Service-USA
P.O. Box 5819
Statesville, NC 28687
800-879-4868
www.hunt-corp.com/office/
xacto/officeframe.html

shells

Editorial Director
Trisha Malcolm

Editor
Colleen Mullaney

Art Director
Chi Ling Moy

Graphic Designer
Caroline Wong

Designer/Stylist
Laura Maffeo

Designer
Mary Helt

Tech Editors
Pam Dailey
Lisa Ventry

Copy Editors
Daryl Brower
Michelle Lo

Photography
Jack Deutsch Studios

•

Book Manager
Cara Beckerich

Production Manager
David Joinnides

**President and Publisher,
Sixth&Spring Books**
Art Joinnides